ANCIENT
AZTECS

BLASTOFF!
DISCOVERY

BY EMILY ROSE OACHS

BELLWETHER MEDIA   MINNEAPOLIS, MN

Blastoff! Discovery launches
a new mission: reading to learn.
Filled with facts and features, each
book offers you an exciting new
world to explore!

This edition first published in 2020 by Bellwether Media, Inc.

No part of this publication may be reproduced in whole or in part
without written permission of the publisher.
For information regarding permission, write to Bellwether Media, Inc.,
Attention: Permissions Department,
6012 Blue Circle Drive, Minnetonka, MN 55343.

Library of Congress Cataloging-in-Publication Data

Names: Oachs, Emily Rose, author.
Title: Ancient Aztecs / By Emily Rose Oachs.
Description: Minneapolis, MN : Bellwether Media, Inc., 2020. |
  Series: Blastoff! Discovery: Ancient civilizations |
    Includes bibliographical references and index. |
  Audience: Ages 7-13 | Audience: Grades 4-6 |
    Summary: "Engaging images accompany information about the
    ancient Aztecs. The combination of high interest subject matter and
    narrative text is intended for students in grades 3 through 8"
    – Provided by publisher.
Identifiers: LCCN 2019036032 (print) | LCCN 2019036033 (ebook)
  | ISBN 9781644871737 (library binding) | ISBN 9781618918574
  (paperback) | ISBN 9781618918499 (ebook)
Subjects: LCSH: Aztecs–History–Juvenile literature. | Aztecs–Social life
  and customs–Juvenile literature. | Mexico–History–Juvenile literature.
Classification: LCC F1219.73 .O23 2020 (print) | LCC F1219.73
  (ebook) | DDC 972–dc23
LC record available at https://lccn.loc.gov/2019036032
LC ebook record available at https://lccn.loc.gov/2019036033

Editor: Kate Moening   Designer: Jeffrey Kollock

Printed in the United States of America, North Mankato, MN.

TABLE OF CONTENTS

THE MARKETPLACE

PLAZA DE LAS TRES CULTURAS, TLATELOLCO

A boy walks toward the open-air Tlatelolco marketplace with his father. They hear a rumble of noise from thousands of people inside. The boy and his father pass by rows of spices, meat, gold jewelry, and feathers. His father stops to hand over **cacao beans** in exchange for corn.

The grand Templo Mayor towers over Tenochtitlán as the boy rushes home. He cannot wait to show his mother their purchases. Market day is always busy in the Aztec Empire!

WHO WERE THE ANCIENT AZTECS?

CEREMONIAL AZTEC OUTFIT

The Aztecs ruled an empire in present-day Mexico from 1325 to 1521. At its height, the empire stretched from the Pacific Ocean to the Atlantic. It ruled around 6 million people. Today, the Aztecs are remembered for their grand cities and fierce warriors.

The largest people group in the empire was the Mexica. In 1325, they founded their famous capital, Tenochtitlán, in the Valley of Mexico. Myths claim they saw an eagle eating a snake on a cactus. They believed this was a sign from the gods to settle there.

ANCIENT TENOCHTITLÁN, MEXICO

THE EAGLE AND THE FLAG

The Mexica story of the eagle eating the snake is still celebrated today. It is the central image on the flag of Mexico!

There were many **city-states** in the Valley of Mexico when the Mexica arrived. The Mexica began to develop vast trading routes around the region. Tenochtitlán's location on Lake Texcoco gave them many items for trade, including fish and frogs.

Growing wealth turned Tenochtitlán into the region's center for religion and trade. Its towering pyramids celebrated the gods. Huge markets brought buyers and sellers from all over. Two **aqueducts** supported the growing population. They carried water from the lake through the city for its citizens.

1519 AZTEC EMPIRE

KEY ▢ Aztec Empire

TEXCOCO

TLACOPAN

TENOCHTITLÁN

MEXICO

N W E S

CHAPULTEPEC AQUEDUCT,
MEXICO CITY

The Valley of Mexico was filled with wetlands and steep hillsides. But the Aztecs' agriculture practices helped their civilization gain strength as the population grew.

CHINAMPAS

The first chinampas in the Valley of Mexico date to before the Aztecs. But the Aztecs' large-scale use of chinampas helped the civilization rise to power. These "floating gardens" are still used in Mexico today!

HOW CHINAMPAS HELPED THE AZTEC EMPIRE GROW

- ☑ increased farmland by converting unusable areas
- ☑ provided more land to build homes
- ☑ increased crop variety for trade with support of up to seven crops each year
- ☑ increased food production to support a growing population

CHINAMPAS

CORN

AVOCADOES

TOMATOES

The Aztecs carved **terraces** into hillsides to create more room for crops. Large **irrigation** systems carried water into fields. On island gardens called *chinampas*, Aztecs grew corn, avocadoes, tomatoes, and many other crops. Chinampas surrounded Tenochtitlán and filled nearby Lakes Chalco and Xochimilco.

HOW THE ANCIENT AZTECS RULED

STATUE OF
TEXCOCO RULER
NEZAHUALCOYOTL

THINK ABOUT IT

What did Tenochtitlán, Texcoco, and Tlacopan have to gain by banding together?

The Aztec Empire was made up of many city-states. Each city-state had a king from its ruling family. A group of four nobles chose an emperor, or *huey tlatoani*, to rule the entire empire from Tenochtitlán.

The city-state Atzcapotzalco controlled Tenochtitlán early on. But in 1428, Tenochtitlán joined forces with Texcoco and the weaker Tlacopan. These city-states formed the Triple **Alliance** and overthrew Atzcapotzalco. Soon, the Triple Alliance took control of large areas of the Valley of Mexico. The Aztec Empire was gaining power.

Warfare strengthened the growing empire. The Triple Alliance grew to control around 500 city-states. The Alliance demanded each city-state give regular **tributes**. These included clothing, rare items, and food. The Aztecs also used warfare to capture prisoners in battle. They offered the prisoners in **sacrifice** to the gods.

People from many different **ethnic** groups lived together under Aztec rule. The major groups included those from the Triple Alliance city-states. These peoples were the Mexica, Acolhua, and Tepaneca.

TENOCHTITLÁN *VS.* TEXCOCO, 1519

KNOWN FOR
religion and military strength

GOVERNMENT
capital of the Aztec Empire and home of the empire's emperor

TENOCHTITLÁN

LOCATION
on an island in Lake Texcoco

POPULATION
more than 200,000 pe

POWER
worked to gain more power over Texcoco and Tlacopan

KNOWN FOR
advanced arts and engineering

GOVERNMENT
city-state governed b king, called a *tlatoar*

TEXCOCO

LOCATION
eastern edge of Lake Texcoco

POPULATION
around 24,000 peop

POWER
worked to stay independent of Tenochtitlán's growing power

Four classes separated Aztec society. The highest was nobility. It included priests, lords, **scribes**, and government and military leaders. Commoners worked as farmers, traders, warriors, and craftsmen. Scribes, craftsmen, and talented warriors were especially important roles. Below commoners were serfs. They lived and worked on nobles' land. Slaves made up the lowest class.

SQUASH

CHILI PEPPERS

CHOCOLATE

Chocolate first came from the Americas. Wealthy Aztecs drank an early version of hot chocolate. It was made from valuable cacao beans.

Aztecs grew their own food or bought food at markets. Corn was a **staple** in Aztec diets. The Aztecs used it to make tamales and tortillas, called *tlaxcalli*. Other common foods included squash, chili peppers, and beans.

Children learned at home until around age 15. Young men then received religious or military training. Young women studied household skills, religious **rituals**, and music. Aztecs' schooling ended when they married.

Young families moved in with the husband's family to raise children. Large extended families of peasants often all lived together. Nobility enjoyed grand, beautiful homes built with stone. Peasants had far simpler houses made of adobe or clay.

AZTEC HOME

ULLAMALIZTLI COURT

THE BALL GAME

The Aztecs often played a ball game called *ullamaliztli*. It was like a mix of basketball and soccer! Players had to get a rubber ball through a ring without using their feet or hands.

19

BELIEFS AND CULTURE

AZTEC RELIGIOUS CEREMONY

The Aztecs believed many gods and goddesses watched over them. Some had also been worshipped by past **Mesoamerican** groups. During religious ceremonies, Aztec priests often practiced human sacrifice. They believed this pleased the gods and prevented the universe's end.

Two calendars guided Aztec life. Their 365-day calendar was based on the sun. The other was a 260-day religious calendar. Every 52 years, the two calendars shared the same first day. On this day, the Aztecs held the New Fire Ceremony. This ensured the world would continue.

AZTEC GODS AND GODDESSES

COATLICUE
- earth goddess of agriculture and childbirth
- mother of Huitzilopochtli

HUITZILOPOCHTLI
- god of war
- protector of Tenochti[tlan]

MICTLANTECUHTLI
- god of the underworld

QUETZALCOATL
- god of learning
- protector of craftsmen

TEZCATLIPOCA
- creator god

TONATIUH
- sun god
- appears on the Aztec Sun[...]

Most Aztecs spoke a language called Nahuatl. Scribes painted the language using **pictographs**. They recorded descriptions of Aztec life, religion, history, and government. Most scribes came from the noble class and were highly educated.

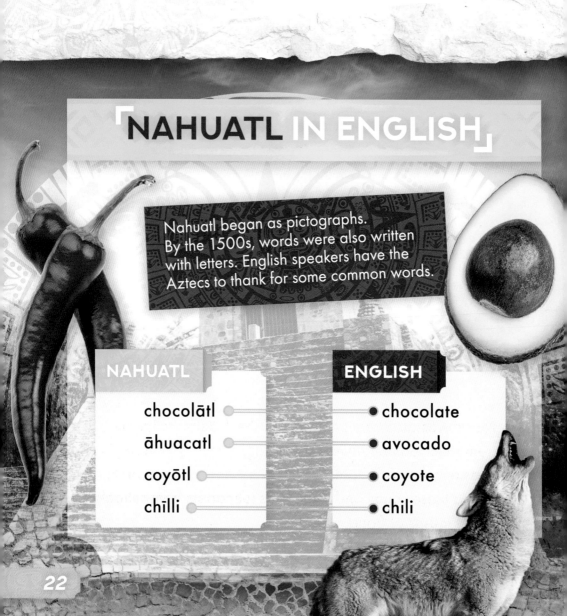

NAHUATL IN ENGLISH

Nahuatl began as pictographs. By the 1500s, words were also written with letters. English speakers have the Aztecs to thank for some common words.

NAHUATL	ENGLISH
chocolātl	chocolate
āhuacatl	avocado
coyōtl	coyote
chīlli	chili

Music was also very important to the Aztecs. Religious ceremonies featured flutes, drumming, dancing, and singing. Songs also helped share Aztec history and myths. Nobility learned these songs and dances as teenagers from schools called Houses of Song.

ᒥAZTEC SUN STONEᒧ

WHO CARVED IT?

craftsman directed by
Aztec emperor Montezuma II

WHEN WAS IT MADE?

early 1500s

WHAT WAS IT?

- carved, circular stone
- features the sun god, Tonatiuh, at its center
- 20 different symbols around the edges stood for each day of the month in the 260-day Aztec calendar
- carvings include jaguars and snakes

WHY WAS IT CREATED?

- honored Tonatiuh
- may have been an altar for priests to perform human sacrifices
- sacrifices honored and fed Tonatiuh to slow down the universe's end

WHERE WAS IT?

Templo Mayor in Tenochtitlán

SIZE

12 feet (3.7 meters) across; more than 40,000 pounds (18,144 kilograms)

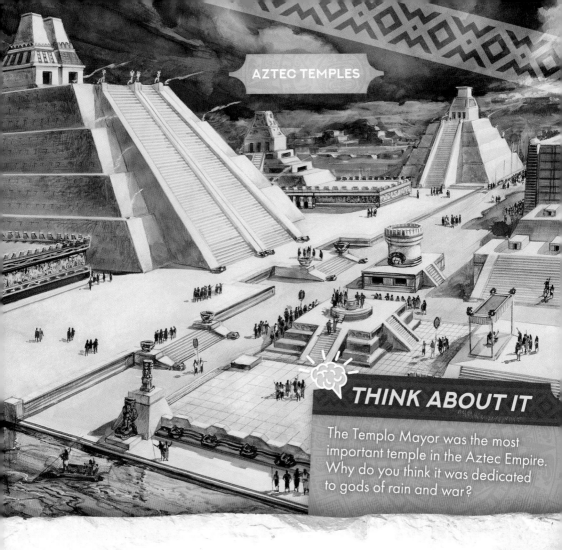

THINK ABOUT IT

The Templo Mayor was the most important temple in the Aztec Empire. Why do you think it was dedicated to gods of rain and war?

Much Aztec art was religious. The detailed Sun Stone honored Tonatiuh. The Aztecs also built beautiful temples to draw favor from the gods. In Tenochtitlán, the Templo Mayor towered about 197 feet (60 meters) tall. It honored the rain god, Tlaloc, and the war god, Huitzilopochtli.

Other art was meant to be worn. Metalworkers made jewelry from silver and gold. Craftsmen created headdresses and shields with valuable feathers from quetzals and other birds. Artists were also known for their detailed sculptures. These often showed the gods or the natural world.

THE FALL OF THE ANCIENT AZTECS

ATZECS BATTLING
THE SPANISH, 1521

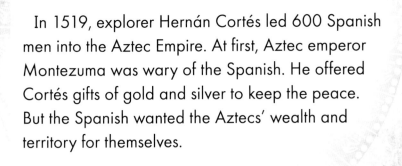

In 1519, explorer Hernán Cortés led 600 Spanish men into the Aztec Empire. At first, Aztec emperor Montezuma was wary of the Spanish. He offered Cortés gifts of gold and silver to keep the peace. But the Spanish wanted the Aztecs' wealth and territory for themselves.

In 1521, the Spanish gathered allies from Tenochtitlán's enemies and rivals. Together, they attacked Tenochtitlán. Tenochtitlán's army fought back, but their spears were no match for Spanish guns. New diseases from Europe also weakened the population. On August 13, the empire fell.

HERNÁN CORTÉS

Few Aztec buildings stand today. The Spanish destroyed Tenochtitlán and built Mexico City in its place. They used stones from the Templo Mayor to build a grand church. But scientists continue to unearth sculptures, pottery, and other **artifacts** from Aztec lands. These help researchers understand Aztec life.

THINK ABOUT IT

Tenochtitlán and its Templo Mayor were important symbols in the Aztec Empire. Why do you think the Spanish decided to destroy them so quickly after the empire fell?

RUINS OF THE TEMPLO MAYOR

AZTEC TIMELINE

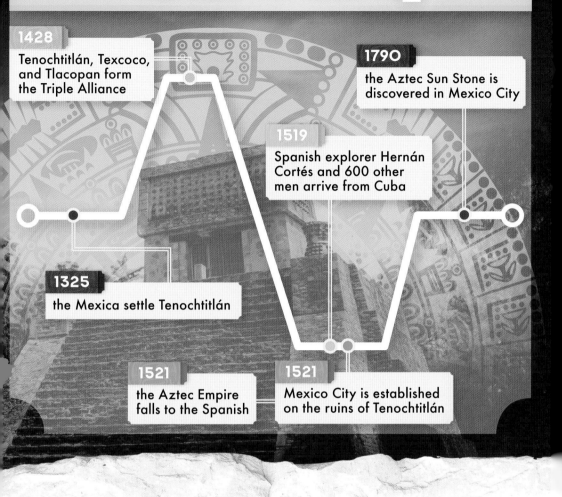

1428
Tenochtitlán, Texcoco, and Tlacopan form the Triple Alliance

1790
the Aztec Sun Stone is discovered in Mexico City

1519
Spanish explorer Hernán Cortés and 600 other men arrive from Cuba

1325
the Mexica settle Tenochtitlán

1521
the Aztec Empire falls to the Spanish

1521
Mexico City is established on the ruins of Tenochtitlán

At least one million Aztec **descendants** still call Mexico home. They even continue some ancient practices. Like the Aztecs, they leave out food and drink during Day of the Dead celebrations. Some tend chinampas. People even speak Nahuatl. Five hundred years after the empire's fall, the Aztec world lives on.

GLOSSARY

alliance—a relationship in which countries or groups of people agree to work together

aqueducts—human-made channels that bring water from one place to another

artifacts—items made long ago by humans; artifacts tell people today about people from the past.

cacao beans—seeds from cacao trees that are used to make chocolate

city-states—self-governing cities and their surrounding areas

descendants—people related to a person or group of people who lived during an earlier time

ethnic—related to a group of people who share customs and an identity

irrigation—the act of bringing water to crops through human-made channels

Mesoamerican—from a region covering central Mexico to El Salvador; groups such as the Aztecs and Maya lived in Mesoamerica before the Spanish arrived.

pictographs—pictures used to communicate in place of words or phrases

rituals—religious ceremonies or practices

sacrifice—an offering of something valuable to please the gods

scribes—people who record information through writing

staple—a widely used food or other item

terraces—flat areas carved into a hill to grow crops

tributes—payments to rulers

TO LEARN MORE

AT THE LIBRARY

Farndon, John. *How to Live Like an Aztec Priest.*
Minneapolis, Minn.: Hungry Tomato, 2016.

Niver, Heather Moore. *Ancient Aztec Daily Life.*
New York, N.Y.: PowerKids Press, 2017.

Williams, Brian. *Maya, Incas, and Aztecs.*
New York, N.Y.: DK Publishing, 2018.

ON THE WEB

FACTSURFER

Factsurfer.com gives you
a safe, fun way to find
more information.

1. Go to www.factsurfer.com.

2. Enter "ancient Aztecs" into the search box
   and click 🔍.

3. Select your book cover to see a list
   of related web sites.

INDEX

The images in this book are reproduced through the courtesy of: aindigo, front cover; Leon Rafael, pp. 3, 24 (sun stone); Diego Grandi, pp. 4-5; Diego Rivera, p. 5; erlucho, p. 6; North Wind Picture Archives/ Alamy, p. 7; javarman, p. 7 (fun fact); Cathyrose Melloan/ Alamy, pp. 8-9; UlrikeStein/ Getty Images, p. 10; Ms_wittaya, p. 10 (corn); Seqoya, p. 11; Akarawut, p. 11 (corn); Vacilando, p. 11 (avocados); Patryk Kosmider, p. 11 (tomatoes); David R. Frazier Photolibrary, Inc./ Alamy, pp. 12-13; Kobby Dagan, p. 13; ChameleonsEye, p. 14; Lev Levin, p. 15; DE AGOSTINI PICTURE LIBRARY/ Getty Images, pp. 16-17, 18; Chatchawal Kittirojana, p. 17 (cocoa); NadyaRa, p. 17 (squash); Sinisa Botas, p. 17 (chili peppers); Vadim Petrakov, pp. 18-19; Francesco Cantone, p. 20; Gwendal Uguen/ Flickr, p. 21; Maks Narodenko, p. 22 (chili); Warren Metcalf, p. 22 (coyote); Kyselova Inna, p. 22 (avocado); DEA / G. DAGLI ORTI/ Getty Images, p. 23; LAFS, p. 24 (landscape); DEA PICTURE LIBRARY/ Getty Images, p. 25; Lebrecht Music & Arts/ Alamy, pp. 26-27; Jose Salamone Pina, p. 27; Luidger, p. 28 (left); Alphonse Pinart, p. 28 (middle); Anagoria, p. 28 (right); WitR, p. 28 (bottom); Bill Perry, p. 31.